A COUNTRYSIDE MISCELLANY

A COUNTRYSIDE MISCELLANY

Summersdale Publishers Ltd
46 West Street
Chichester
West Sussex
PO19 1RP
UK

www.summersdale.com

Printed and bound in China

ISBN: 978-1-84953-568-7

Substantial discounts on bulk quantities of Summersdale books are available to corporations, professional associations and other organisations. For details contact Nicky Douglas by telephone: +44 (0) 1243 756902, fax: +44 (0) 1243 786300 or email: nicky@summersdale.com.

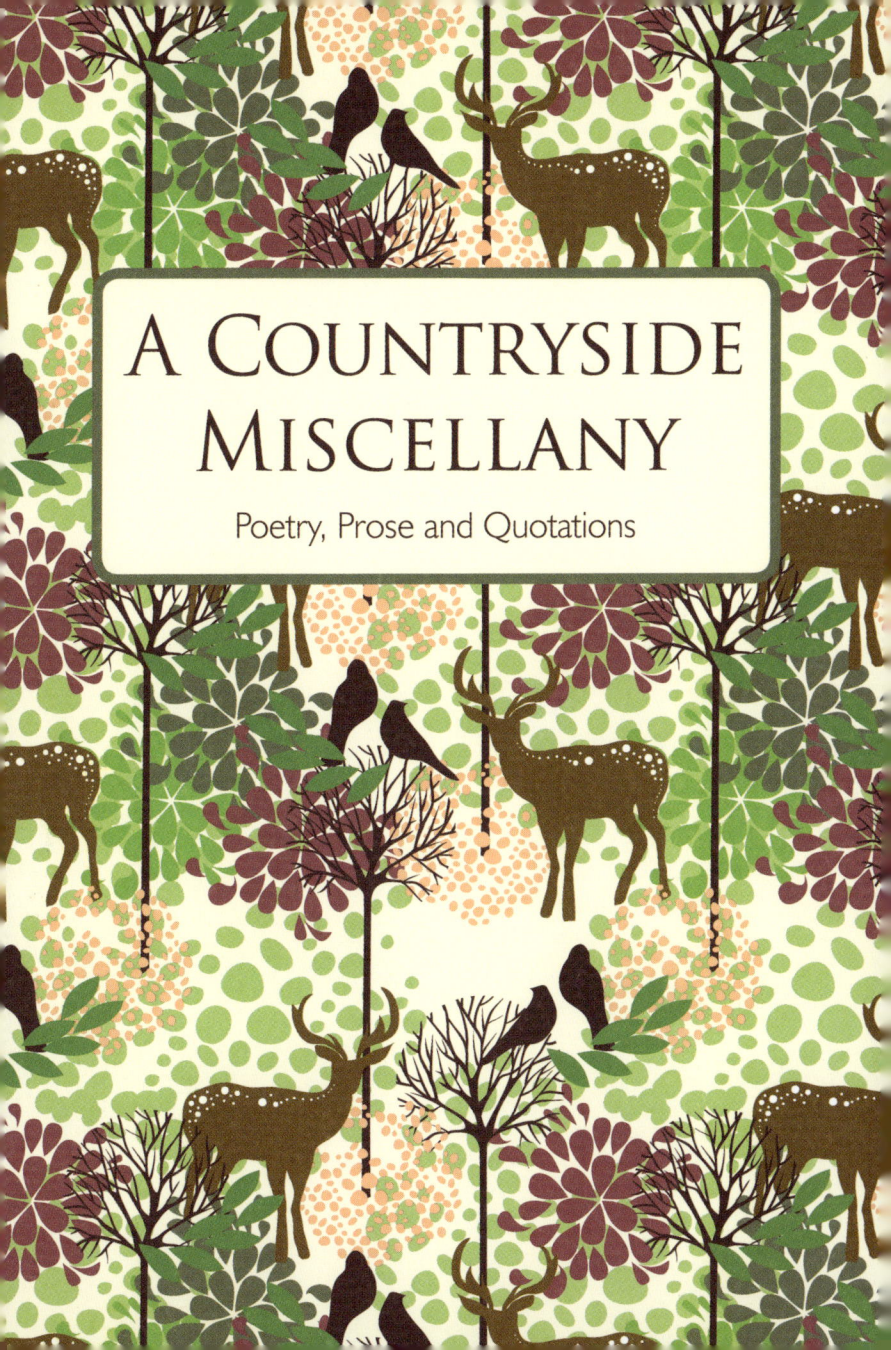

A COUNTRYSIDE MISCELLANY

Poetry, Prose and Quotations

CONTENTS

Goldenrod and asters fringed the mossy walls. Grasshoppers skipped briskly in the sere grass, and crickets chirped like fairy pipers at a feast. Squirrels were busy with their small harvesting. Birds twittered their adieux from the alders in the lane, and every tree stood ready to send down its shower of red or yellow apples at the first shake.

LOUISA MAY ALCOTT, *LITTLE WOMEN*

The trip was like riding through a long picture gallery, full of lovely landscapes. The farmhouses were my delight, with thatched roofs, ivy up to the eaves, latticed windows, and stout women with rosy children at the doors. The very cattle looked more tranquil than ours, as they stood knee-deep in clover, and the hens had a contented cluck, as if they never got nervous like Yankee biddies. Such perfect colour I never saw, the grass so green, sky so blue, grain so yellow, woods so dark, I was in a rapture all the way.

LOUISA MAY ALCOTT, *LITTLE WOMEN*

Sunshine in February

O winter Sun!

How beautiful thy beams

Upon the chainèd earth!

The snows are melting and the gale

Is hushed; thou shinest, soft and pale,

O Winter Sun!

Upon a world that dreams,

And trembles with awakened hopes of birth.

O Joyful Green!

'Mid snowy patches gay

Thou peerest, and the sky

Shines blue through twiggèd boughs; each tree

Is aching now with thoughts of thee,

O Joyful Green!

Spring's heart is in the day

Though Winter's hands upon night's bosom lie.

LAURENCE ALMA-TADEMA

The Grasshopper

Happy insect! what can be
In happiness compar'd to thee?
Fed with nourishment divine,
The dewy morning's gentle wine!
Nature waits upon thee still,
And thy verdant cup does fill;
'Tis filled wherever thou dost tread,
Nature self's thy Ganymede.
Thou dost drink, and dance, and sing;
Happier than the happiest king!
All the fields which thou dost see,
All the plants belong to thee;
All that summer hours produce;
Fertile made with early juice.
Man for thee does sow and plow;
Farmer he, and landlord thou!
Thou dost innocently joy;

Nor does thy luxury destroy;
The shepherd gladly heareth thee,
More harmonious than he.
Thee country hinds with gladness hear,
Prophet of the ripen'd year!
Thee Phoebus loves, and does inspire;
Phoebus is himself thy sire.
To thee, of all things upon earth,
Life's no longer than thy mirth.
Happy insect, happy, thou
Dost neither age nor winter know;
But, when thou'st drunk, and danc'd and sung
Thy fill, the flowery leaves among,
(Voluptuous and wise withal,
Epicurean animal!) –
Sated with thy summer feast,
Thou retir'st to endless rest.

ANACREON

And meanwhile the beautiful golden days were dropping gently from the second week one by one, equal in beauty with those of the first, and the scent of beanfields in flower on the hillside behind the village came across to San Salvatore whenever the air moved… Everything seemed to be out together – all the things crowded into one month which in England are spread penuriously over six. Even primroses were found one day by Mrs Wilkins in a cold corner up in the hills; and when she brought them down to the geraniums and heliotrope of San Salvatore they looked quite shy.

ELIZABETH VON ARNIM, *THE ENCHANTED APRIL*

In Meryton they parted; the two youngest repaired to the lodgings of one of the officers' wives, and Elizabeth continued her walk alone, crossing field after field at a quick pace, jumping over stiles and springing over puddles with impatient activity, and finding herself at last within view of the house, with weary ankles, dirty stockings, and a face glowing with the warmth of exercise.

JANE AUSTEN, *PRIDE AND PREJUDICE*

The whole country about them abounded in beautiful walks. The high downs which invited them from almost every window of the cottage to seek the exquisite enjoyment of air on their summits, were a happy alternative when the dirt of the valleys beneath shut up their superior beauties; and towards one of these hills did Marianne and Margaret one memorable morning direct their steps, attracted by the partial sunshine of a showery sky, and unable longer to bear the confinement which the settled rain of the two preceding days had occasioned. The weather was not tempting enough to draw the two others from their pencil and their book, in spite of Marianne's declaration that the day would be lastingly fair, and that every threatening cloud would be drawn off from their hills; and the two girls set off together.

They gaily ascended the downs, rejoicing in their own penetration at every glimpse of blue sky; and when they caught in their faces the animating gales of a high south-westerly wind, they pitied the fears which had prevented their mother and Elinor from sharing such delightful sensations.

'Is there a felicity in the world,' said Marianne, 'superior to this? – Margaret, we will walk here at least two hours.'

JANE AUSTEN, *SENSE AND SENSIBILITY*

from Aurora Leigh

I dared to rest, or wander, – like a rest
Made sweeter for the step upon the grass, –
And view the ground's most gentle dimplement,
(As if God's finger touched but did not press
In making England!) such an up and down
Of verdure, – nothing too much up or down,
A ripple of land; such little hills, the sky
Can stoop to tenderly and the wheatfields climb;
Such nooks of valleys, lined with orchises,
Fed full of noises by invisible streams;
And open pastures, where you scarcely tell
White daisies from white dew, – at intervals
The mythic oaks and elm-trees standing out
Self-poised upon their prodigy of shade, –
I thought my father's land was worthy too
Of being my Shakespeare's.

ELIZABETH BARRETT BROWNING

Flowers have an expression of countenance as much as men or animals. Some seem to smile; some have a sad expression; some are pensive and diffident; others again are plain, honest and upright, like the broad-faced sunflower and the hollyhock.

HENRY WARD BEECHER, *STAR PAPERS*

from Spring

Sound the flute!
Now it's mute.
Bird's delight,
Day and night;
Nightingale,
In the dale,
Lark in sky,
Merrily,
Merrily merrily, to welcome in the year.

[...]

Little lamb,
Here I am;
Come and lick
My white neck;
Let me pull
Your soft wool;
Let me kiss
Your soft face;
Merrily, merrily, we welcome in the year.

WILLIAM BLAKE

April Rain

The April rain, the April rain,
Comes slanting down in fitful showers,
Then from the furrow shoots the grain,
And banks are fledged with nestling flowers;
And in grey shaw and woodland bowers
The cuckoo through the April rain
Calls once again.

The April sun, the April sun,
Glints through the rain in fitful splendour,
And in grey shaw and woodland dun
The little leaves spring forth and tender
Their infant hands, yet weak and slender,
For warmth towards the April sun,
One after one.

And between shower and shine hath birth

The rainbow's evanescent glory;

Heaven's light that breaks on mists of earth!

Frail symbol of our human story,

It flowers through showers where, looming hoary,

The rain-clouds flash with April mirth,

Like Life on earth.

MATHILDE BLIND

I have a very pleasant recollection of that walk, along the hard, white, sunny road, shaded here and there with bright green trees, and adorned with flowery banks and blossoming hedges of delicious fragrance; or through pleasant fields and lanes, all glorious in the sweet flowers and brilliant verdure of delightful May.

ANNE BRONTË, *THE TENANT OF WILDFELL HALL*

Not many days after this, on a mild sunny morning – rather soft under foot; for the last fall of snow was only just wasted away, leaving yet a thin ridge, here and there, lingering on the fresh green grass beneath the hedges; but beside them already, the young primroses were peeping from among their moist, dark foliage, and the lark above was singing of summer, and hope, and love, and every heavenly thing – I was out on the hillside, enjoying these delights, and looking after the well-being of my young lambs and their mothers, when, on glancing round me, I beheld three persons ascending from the vale below.

ANNE BRONTË, *THE TENANT OF WILDFELL HALL*

It was three o'clock; the church bell tolled as I passed under the belfry: the charm of the hour lay in its approaching dimness, in the low-gliding and pale-beaming sun. I was a mile from Thornfield, in a lane noted for wild roses in summer, for nuts and blackberries in autumn, and even now possessing a few coral treasures in hips and haws, but whose best winter delight lay in its utter solitude and leafless repose. If a breath of air stirred, it made no sound here; for there was not a holly, not an evergreen to rustle, and the stripped hawthorn and hazel bushes were as still as the white, worn stones which causewayed the middle of the path. Far and wide, on each side, there were only fields, where no cattle now browsed; and the little brown birds, which stirred occasionally in the hedge, looked like single russet leaves that had forgotten to drop.

CHARLOTTE BRONTË, *JANE EYRE*

He said the pleasantest manner of spending a hot July day was lying from morning till evening on a bank of heath in the middle of the moors, with the bees humming dreamily about among the bloom, and the larks singing high up overhead, and the blue sky and bright sun shining steadily and cloudlessly. That was his most perfect idea of heaven's happiness: mine was rocking in a rustling green tree, with a west wind blowing, and bright white clouds flitting rapidly above; and not only larks, but throstles, and blackbirds, and linnets, and cuckoos pouring out music on every side, and the moors seen at a distance, broken into cool dusky dells; but close by great swells of long grass undulating in waves to the breeze; and woods and sounding water, and the whole world awake and wild with joy. He wanted all to lie in an ecstasy of peace; I wanted all to sparkle and dance in a glorious jubilee. I said his heaven would be only half alive; and he said mine would be drunk: I said I should fall asleep in his; and he said he could not breathe in mine, and began to grow very snappish. At last, we agreed to try both, as soon as the right weather came.

EMILY BRONTË, *WUTHERING HEIGHTS*

from Song III

There is no one season such delight can bring
As summer, autumn, winter and the spring.

WILLIAM BROWNE

Home Thoughts, from Abroad

O, to be in England
Now that April's there,
And whoever wakes in England
Sees, some morning, unaware,
That the lowest boughs and the brushwood sheaf
Round the elm-tree bole are in tiny leaf,
While the chaffinch sings on the orchard bough
In England – now!

And after April, when May follows,
And the whitethroat builds, and all the swallows!
Hark, where my blossom'd pear-tree in the hedge
Leans to the field and scatters on the clover
Blossoms and dewdrops – at the bent spray's edge –
That's the wise thrush; he sings each song twice over,
Lest you should think he never could recapture
The first fine careless rapture!
And though the fields look rough with hoary dew,
All will be gay when noontide wakes anew
The buttercups, the little children's dower –
Far brighter than this gaudy melon-flower!

ROBERT BROWNING

'He knows all about eggs and nests,' Mary went on. 'And he knows where foxes and badgers and otters live. He keeps them secret so that other boys won't find their holes and frighten them. He knows about everything that grows or lives on the moor.'

'Does he like the moor?' said Colin. 'How can he when it's such a great, bare, dreary place?'

'It's the most beautiful place,' protested Mary. 'Thousands of lovely things grow on it and there are thousands of little creatures all busy building nests and making holes and burrows and chippering or singing or squeaking to each other. They are so busy and having such fun under the earth or in the trees or heather. It's their world… When Dickon talks about it you feel as if you saw things and heard them and as if you were standing in the heather with the sun shining and the gorse smelling like honey – and all full of bees and butterflies.'

FRANCES HODGSON BURNETT, *THE SECRET GARDEN*

There is scarcely any earthly object that gives me more – I don't know if I should call it pleasure, but something which exalts me, something which enraptures me – than to walk in the sheltered side of a wood or high plantation, in a cloudy winter day, and hear a stormy wind howling among the trees and raving o'er the plain.

ROBERT BURNS, 'MEMORANDA'

The Gladness of Nature

Is this a time to be cloudy and sad,
When our mother Nature laughs around;
When even the deep blue heavens look glad,
And gladness breathes from
the blossoming ground?

There are notes of joy from the
hang-bird and wren,
And the gossip of swallows through all the sky;
The ground-squirrel gaily chirps by his den,
And the wilding bee hums merrily by.

The clouds are at play in the azure space,
And their shadows at play on
the bright green vale,
And here they stretch to the frolic chase,
And there they roll on the easy gale.

There's a dance of leaves in that aspen bower,
There's a titter of winds in that beechen tree,
There's a smile on the fruit, and
a smile on the flower,
And a laugh from the brook that runs to the sea.

And look at the broad-faced sun, how he smiles
On the dewy earth that smiles in his ray,
On the leaping waters and gay young isles;
Ay, look, and he'll smile thy gloom away.

WILLIAM CULLEN BRYANT

from Solitude

To sit on rocks, to muse o'er flood and fell,

To slowly trace the forest's shady scene,

Where things that own not man's dominion dwell,

And mortal foot hath ne'er or rarely been;

To climb the trackless mountain all unseen,

With the wild flock that never needs a fold;

Alone o'er steeps and foaming falls to lean;

This is not solitude, 'tis but to hold

Converse with Nature's charms,

and view her stores unrolled.

LORD BYRON

Autumn Birds

The wild duck startles like a sudden thought,
And heron slow as if it might be caught.
The flopping crows on weary wings go by
And grey beard jackdaws noising as they fly.
The crowds of starnels whizz and hurry by,
And darken like a cloud the evening sky.
The larks like thunder rise and suthy round,
Then drop and nestle in the stubble ground.
The wild swan hurries hight and noises loud
With white neck peering to the evening clowd.
The weary rooks to distant woods are gone.
With lengths of tail the magpie winnows on
To neighbouring tree, and leaves the distant crow
While small birds nestle in the edge below.

JOHN CLARE

On a Lane in Spring

A little lane – the brook runs close beside,
And spangles in the sunshine, while the fish
glide swiftly by;
And hedges leafing with the green springtide;
From out their greenery the old birds fly,
And chirp and whistle in the morning sun;
The pilewort glitters 'neath the pale blue sky,
The little robin has its nest begun
The grass-green linnets round the bushes fly.
How mild the spring comes in! the daisy buds
Lift up their golden blossoms to the sky.
How lovely are the pingles in the woods!
Here a beetle runs – and there a fly
Rests on the arum leaf in bottle-green,
And all the spring in this sweet lane is seen.

JOHN CLARE

from The Moon, how definite its orb!

The Moon, how definite its orb!
Yet gaze again, and with a steady gaze –
'Tis there indeed, – but where is it not? –
It is suffused o'er all the sapphire Heaven,
Trees, herbage, snake-like
stream, unwrinkled Lake,
Whose very murmur does of it partake
And low and close the broad smooth mountain
Is more a thing of Heaven than when
Distinct by one dim shade and yet
undivided from the universal cloud
In which it towers, finite in height.

SAMUEL TAYLOR COLERIDGE

The Months

January brings the snow,
Makes our feet and fingers glow.

February brings the rain,
Thaws the frozen lake again.

March brings breezes loud and shrill,
Stirs the dancing daffodil.

April brings the primrose sweet,
Scatters daises at our feet.

May brings flocks of pretty lambs,
Skipping by their fleecy dams.

June brings tulips, lilies, roses,
Fills the children's hands with posies.

Hot July brings cooling showers,
Apricots and gillyflowers.

August brings the sheaves of corn,
Then the harvest home is borne.

Warm September brings the fruit,
Sportsmen then begin to shoot.

Fresh October brings the pheasant,
Then to gather nuts is pleasant.

Dull November brings the blast,
Then the leaves are whirling fast.

Chill December brings the sleet,
Blazing fire, and Christmas treat.

SARA COLERIDGE

for the leaping greenly spirits of
trees and a blue dream of sky;and
for everything which is natural

E. E. CUMMINGS

I came into the valley, as the evening sun was shining on the remote heights of snow, that closed it in, like eternal clouds. The bases of the mountains forming the gorge in which the little village lay, were richly green; and high above this gentler vegetation, grew forests of dark fir, cleaving the wintry snow-drift, wedge-like, and stemming the avalanche. Above these, were range upon range of craggy steeps, grey rock, bright ice, and smooth verdure-specks of pasture, all gradually blending with the crowning snow… So did even the clustered village in the valley, with its wooden bridge across the stream, where the stream tumbled over broken rocks, and roared away among the trees.

CHARLES DICKENS, *DAVID COPPERFIELD*

Oliver rose next morning, in better heart, and went about his usual occupations, with more hope and pleasure than he had known for many days. The birds were once more hung out, to sing, in their old places; and the sweetest wild flowers that could be found, were once more gathered to gladden Rose with their beauty. The melancholy which had seemed to the sad eyes of the anxious boy to hang, for days past, over every object, beautiful as all were, was dispelled by magic. The dew seemed to sparkle more brightly on the green leaves; the air to rustle among them with a sweeter music; and the sky itself to look more blue and bright. Such is the influence which the condition of our own thoughts, exercise, even over the appearance of external objects. Men who look on nature, and their fellow-men, and cry that all is dark and gloomy, are in the right; but the sombre colours are reflections from their own jaundiced eyes and hearts. The real hues are delicate, and need a clearer vision.

CHARLES DICKENS, *OLIVER TWIST*

A Bird Came Down

A bird came down the walk:
He did not know I saw;
He bit an angle-worm in halves
And ate the fellow, raw.

And then he drank a dew
From a convenient grass,
And then hopped sidewise to the wall
To let a beetle pass.

He glanced with rapid eyes
That hurried all abroad, –
They looked like frightened beads, I thought;
He stirred his velvet head

Like one in danger; cautious,
    I offered him a crumb,
And he unrolled his feathers
And rowed him softer home

Than oars divide the ocean,
    Too silver for a seam,
Or butterflies, off banks of noon,
Leap, splashless, as they swim.

EMILY DICKINSON

Nature – the Gentlest Mother is,

Nature – the Gentlest Mother is,
Impatient of no Child –
The feeblest – or the waywardest –
Her Admonition mild –

In Forest – and the Hill –
By Traveller – be heard –
Restraining Rampant Squirrel –
Or too impetuous Bird –

How fair Her Conversation –
A Summer Afternoon –
Her Household – Her Assembly –
And when the Sun go down –

Her Voice among the Aisles

Incite the timid prayer

Of the minutest Cricket –

The most unworthy Flower –

When all the Children sleep –

She turns as long away

As will suffice to light Her lamps –

Then bending from the Sky –

With infinite Affection –

And infiniter Care –

Her Golden finger on Her lip –

Wills Silence – Everywhere –

EMILY DICKINSON

The whole earth was brimming
sunshine that morning. She tripped
along, the clear sky pouring
liquid blue into her soul.

THEODORE DREISER, *SISTER CARRIE*

Deer

Shy in their herding dwell the fallow deer.
They are spirits of wild sense. Nobody near
Comes upon their pastures.
There a life they live,
Of sufficient beauty, phantom, fugitive,
Treading as in jungles free leopards do,
Printless as evelight, instant as dew.
The great kine are patient, and
home-coming sheep
Know our bidding. The fallow deer keep
Delicate and far their counsels wild,
Never to be folded reconciled
To the spoiling hand as the poor flocks are;
Lightfoot, and swift, and unfamiliar,
These you may not hinder, unconfined
Beautiful flocks of the mind.

JOHN DRINKWATER

A wide plain, where the broadening Floss hurries on between its green banks to the sea, and the loving tide, rushing to meet it, checks its passage with an impetuous embrace... Far away on each hand stretch the rich pastures, and the patches of dark earth made ready for the seed of broad-leaved green crops, or touched already with the tint of the tender-bladed autumn-sown corn. There is a remnant still of last year's golden clusters of beehive-ricks rising at intervals beyond the hedgerows; and everywhere the hedgerows are studded with trees; the distant ships seem to be lifting their masts and stretching their red-brown sails close among the branches of the spreading ash. Just by the red-roofed town the tributary Ripple flows with a lively current into the Floss. How lovely the little river is, with its dark changing wavelets! It seems to me like a living companion while I wander along the bank, and listen to its low, placid voice, as to the voice of one who is deaf and loving. I remember those large dipping willows. I remember the stone bridge.

GEORGE ELIOT, *THE MILL ON THE FLOSS*

The Twelve Months

Snowy, Flowy, Blowy,
Showery, Flowery, Bowery,
Hoppy, Croppy, Droppy,
Breezy, Sneezy, Freezy.

GEORGE ELLIS

from To Ellen at the South

The green grass is bowing,
The morning wind is in it;
'Tis a tune worth thy knowing,
Though it change every minute.

'Tis a tune of the Spring;
Every year plays it over
To the robin on the wing,
And to the pausing lover.

O'er ten thousand, thousand acres,
Goes light the nimble zephyr;
The Flowers – tiny sect of Shakers –
Worship him ever.

RALPH WALDO EMERSON

Xenophanes

By fate, not option, frugal Nature gave
One scent to hyson and to wall-flower,
One sound to pine-groves and to waterfalls,
One aspect to the desert and the lake.
It was her stern necessity: all things
Are of one pattern made; bird, beast and flower,
Song, picture, form, space, thought and character
Deceive us, seeming to be many things,
And are but one. Beheld far off, they part
As God and devil; bring them to the mind,
They dull its edge with their monotony.
To know one element, explore another,
And in the second reappears the first.
The specious panorama of a year
But multiplies the image of a day,—
A belt of mirrors round a taper's flame;
And universal Nature, through her vast
And crowded whole, an infinite paroquet,
Repeats one note.

RALPH WALDO EMERSON

English Hills

O that I were
Where breaks the pure cold light
On English hills,
And peewits rising cry,
And grey is all the sky.

Or at evening there
When the faint slow light stays,
And far below
Sleeps the last lingering sound,
And night leans all round.

O then, O there
'Tis English haunted ground.
The diligent stars
Creep out, watch, and smile;
The wise moon lingers awhile.

For surely there
Heroic shapes are moving,
Visible thoughts,
Passions, things divine,
Clear beneath clear star-shine.

O that I were
Again on English hills,
Seeing between
Laborious villages
Her cool dark loveliness.

JOHN FREEMAN

November Skies

Than these November skies
Is no sky lovelier. The clouds are deep;
Into their grey the subtle spies
Of colour creep,
Changing that high austerity to delight,
Till ev'n the leaden interfolds are bright.
And, where the cloud breaks, faint far azure peers
Ere a thin flushing cloud again
Shuts up that loveliness, or shares.
The huge great clouds move slowly, gently, as
Reluctant the quick sun should shine in vain,
Holding in bright caprice their rain.
And when of colours none,
Not rose, nor amber, nor the scarce late green,
Is truly seen, –
In all the myriad grey,
In silver height and dusky deep, remain
The loveliest,
Faint purple flushes of the unvanquished sun.

John Freeman

The Wild Honey Suckle

Fair flower, that dost so comely grow,
Hid in this silent, dull retreat,
Untouched thy honied blossoms blow,
Unseen thy little branches greet:
No roving foot shall crush thee here,
No busy hand provoke a tear.

By Nature's self in white arrayed,
She bade thee shun the vulgar eye,
And planted here the guardian shade,
And sent soft waters murmuring by;
Thus quietly thy summer goes,
Thy days declining to repose,

Smit with those charms, that must decay,
I grieve to see your future doom;
They died – nor were those flowers more gay,
The flowers that did in Eden bloom;
Unpitying frosts, and Autumn's power
Shall leave no vestige of this flower.

From morning suns and evening dews
At first thy little being came:
If nothing once, you nothing lose,
For when you die you are the same;
The space between, is but an hour,
The frail duration of a flower.

PHILIP FRENEAU

There had been rain the night before – a spring rain, and the earth smelt of sap and wild grasses. The warm, soft breeze swung the leaves and the golden buds of the old oak tree, and in the sunshine the blackbirds were whistling their hearts out.

It was such a spring day as breathes into a man an ineffable yearning, a painful sweetness, a longing that makes him stand motionless, looking at the leaves or grass, and fling out his arms to embrace he knows not what. The earth gave forth a fainting warmth, stealing up through the chilly garment in which winter had wrapped her.

JOHN GALSWORTHY, *THE MAN OF PROPERTY*

I remember a hundred lovely lakes, and recall the fragrant breath of pine and fir and cedar and poplar trees. The trail has strung upon it, as upon a thread of silk, opalescent dawns and saffron sunsets. It has given me blessed release from care and worry and the troubled thinking of our modern day. It has been a return to the primitive and the peaceful. Whenever the pressure of our complex city life thins my blood and benumbs my brain, I seek relief in the trail.

HAMLIN GARLAND, 'HITTING THE TRAIL'

Ruth and Mr Bellingham plunged through the broken ground to regain the road near the wayside inn. Hand-in-hand, now pricked by the far-spreading gorse, now ankle-deep in sand; now pressing the soft, thick heath, which should make so brave an autumn show; and now over wild thyme and other fragrant herbs, they made their way, with many a merry laugh. Once on the road, at the summit, Ruth stood silent, in breathless delight at the view before her. The hill fell suddenly down into the plain, extending for a dozen miles or more. There was a clump of dark Scotch firs close to them, which cut clear against the western sky, and threw back the nearest levels into distance. The plain below them was richly wooded, and was tinted by the young tender hues of the earliest summer, for all the trees of the wood had donned their leaves except the cautious ash, which here and there gave a soft, pleasant greyness to the landscape… The view was bounded by some rising ground in deep purple shadow against the sunset sky.

ELIZABETH GASKELL, *RUTH*

Their breakfast-hour was late, in accordance with Mr Bellingham's tastes and habits; but Ruth was up betimes, and out and away, brushing the dew-drops from the short crisp grass; the lark sung high above her head, and she knew not if she moved or stood still, for the grandeur of this beautiful earth absorbed all idea of separate and individual existence. Even rain was a pleasure to her... she saw the swift-fleeting showers come athwart the sunlight like a rush of silver arrows; she watched the purple darkness on the heathery mountain-side, and then the pale golden gleam which succeeded. There was no change or alteration of nature that had not its own peculiar beauty in the eyes of Ruth.

ELIZABETH GASKELL, *RUTH*

Forget not that the earth delights to feel your bare feet and the winds long to play with your hair.

Kahlil Gibran, *The Prophet*

An Invitation

Come to the river-bank with me;
For there are plumed ferns of crescent green,
And in the wine-dark pools are seen
The crimson-spotted trout.
Hush! hush! move through the
brake most silently,
Vex with no loud unhallow'd shout
The holy secrecy of this sweet glade,
And you shall see
The dipper rush with sudden flash, and fade
Into the woodland screen;
Nor shall you by your presence make afraid
The kingfisher, who looks down dreamily
At his own shadow gorgeously array'd.

EDMUND GOSSE

I t all seemed too good to be true. Hither and thither through the meadows he rambled busily, along the hedgerows, across the copses, finding everywhere birds building, flowers budding, leaves thrusting – everything happy, and progressive, and occupied...

He thought his happiness was complete when, as he meandered aimlessly along, suddenly he stood by the edge of a full-fed river. Never in his life had he seen a river before – this sleek, sinuous, full-bodied animal, chasing and chuckling, gripping things with a gurgle and leaving them with a laugh, to fling itself on fresh playmates that shook themselves free, and were caught and held again. All was a-shake and a-shiver – glints and gleams and sparkles, rustle and swirl, chatter and bubble. The Mole was bewitched, entranced, fascinated. By the side of the river he trotted as one trots, when very small, by the side of a man who holds one spell-bound by exciting stories; and when tired at last, he sat on the bank, while the river still chattered on to him, a babbling procession of the best stories in the world, sent from the heart of the earth to be told at last to the insatiable sea.

KENNETH GRAHAME, *THE WIND IN THE WILLOWS*

Drowsy animals, snug in their holes while wind and rain were battering at their doors, recalled still keen mornings, an hour before sunrise, when the white mist, as yet undispersed, clung closely along the surface of the water; then the shock of the early plunge, the scamper along the bank, and the radiant transformation of earth, air, and water, when suddenly the sun was with them again, and grey was gold and colour was born and sprang out of the earth once more. They recalled the languorous siesta of hot mid-day, deep in green undergrowth, the sun striking through in tiny golden shafts and spots; the boating and bathing of the afternoon, the rambles along dusty lanes and through yellow corn-fields; and the long, cool evening at last, when so many threads were gathered up, so many friendships rounded, and so many adventures planned for the morrow.

KENNETH GRAHAME, *THE WIND IN THE WILLOWS*

I Watched a Blackbird

I watched a blackbird on a budding sycamore
One Easter Day, when sap was stirring twigs to
the core;
I saw his tongue, and crocus-coloured bill
Parting and closing as he turned his trill;
Then he flew down, seized on a stem of hay,
And upped to where his building scheme was
under way,
As if so sure a nest were never
shaped on spray.

Thomas Hardy

The Darkling Thrush

I leant upon a coppice gate
When Frost was spectre-grey,
And Winter's dregs made desolate
The weakening eye of day.
The tangled bine-stems scored the sky
Like strings of broken lyres,
And all mankind that haunted nigh
Had sought their household fires.

The land's sharp features seemed to be
The Century's corpse outleant,
His crypt the cloudy canopy,
The wind his death-lament.
The ancient pulse of germ and birth
Was shrunken hard and dry,
And every spirit upon earth
Seemed fervourless as I.

At once a voice arose among
The bleak twigs overhead
In a full-hearted evensong
Of joy illimited;
An aged thrush, frail, gaunt and small,
In blast-beruffled plume,
Had chosen thus to fling his soul
Upon the growing gloom.

So little cause for carolings
Of such ecstatic sound
Was written on terrestrial things
Afar or nigh around,
That I could think there trembled through
His happy good-night air
Some blessed Hope, whereof he knew
And I was unaware.

THOMAS HARDY

Here they sat down on a luxuriant heap of moss; which at some epoch of the preceding century, had been a gigantic pine, with its roots and trunk in the darksome shade, and its head aloft in the upper atmosphere. It was a little dell where they had seated themselves, with a leaf-strewn bank rising gently on either side, and a brook flowing through the midst, over a bed of fallen and drowned leaves. The trees impending over it had flung down great branches from time to time, which choked up the current, and compelled it to form eddies and black depths at some points; while, in its swifter and livelier passages there appeared a channel-way of pebbles, and brown, sparkling sand. Letting the eyes follow along the course of the stream, they could catch the reflected light from its water, at some short distance within the forest, but soon lost all traces of it amid the bewilderment of tree-trunks and underbrush, and here and there a huge rock covered over with grey lichens. All these giant trees and boulders of granite seemed intent on making a mystery of the course of this small brook; fearing, perhaps, that, with its never-ceasing loquacity, it should whisper tales out of the heart of the old forest whence it flowed, or mirror its revelations on the smooth surface of a pool. Continually, indeed, as it stole onward, the streamlet kept up a babble, kind, quiet, soothing, but melancholy, like the voice of a young child that was spending its infancy without playfulness, and knew not how to be merry among sad acquaintance and events of sombre hue.

NATHANIEL HAWTHORNE, *THE SCARLET LETTER*

from Pastoral

It's the Spring.
Earth has conceived, and her bosom,
Teeming with summer, is glad.

Vistas of change and adventure,
Thro' the green land
The grey roads go beckoning and winding,
Peopled with wains, and melodious
With harness-bells jangling:
Jangling and twangling rough rhythms
To the slow march of the stately, great horses
Whistled and shouted along.

White fleets of cloud,
Argosies heavy with fruitfulness,
Sail the blue peacefully. Green flame the hedgerows.
Blackbirds are bugling, and white in wet winds
Sway the tall poplars.
Pageants of colour and fragrance,
Pass the sweet meadows, and viewless
Walks the mild spirit of May,
Visibly blessing the world.

O, the brilliance of blossoming orchards!
O, the savour and thrill of the woods,
When their leafage is stirred
By the flight of the Angel of Rain!
Loud lows the steer; in the fallows
Rooks are alert; and the brooks
Gurgle and tinkle and trill. Thro' the gloamings,
Under the rare, shy stars,
Boy and girl wander
Dreaming in darkness and dew.

WILLIAM ERNEST HENLEY

To Daffodils

Fair daffodils, we weep to see
You haste away so soon.
As yet the early-rising sun
Hath not attain'd his noon.
Stay, stay,
Until the hasting day
Has run
But to the even-song;
And, having pray'd together, we
Will go with you along.

We have short time to stay, as you;
We have as short a spring;
As quick a growth to meet decay,
As you, or any thing.
We die.
As your hours do, and dry
Away
Like to the summer's rain;
Or as the pearls of morning's dew
Ne'er to be found again.

<small>Robert Herrick</small>

October's Bright Blue Weather

O suns and skies and clouds of June,
And flowers of June together,
Ye cannot rival for one hour
October's bright blue weather;

When loud the bumblebee makes haste,
Belated, thriftless vagrant,
And goldenrod is dying fast,
And lanes with grapes are fragrant;

When gentians roll their fingers tight
To save them for the morning,
And chestnuts fall from satin burrs
Without a sound of warning;

When on the ground red apples lie
In piles like jewels shining,
And redder still on old stone walls
Are leaves of woodbine twining;

When all the lovely wayside things
Their white-winged seeds are sowing,
And in the fields still green and fair,
Late aftermaths are growing;

When springs run low, and on the brooks,
In idle golden freighting,
Bright leaves sink noiseless in the hush
Of woods, for winter waiting;

When comrades seek sweet country haunts,
By twos and twos together,
And count like misers, hour by hour,
October's bright blue weather.

O sun and skies and flowers of June,
Count all your boasts together,
Love loveth best of all the year
October's bright blue weather.

HELEN HUNT JACKSON

The great charm, however, of English scenery, is the moral feeling that seems to pervade it. It is associated in the mind with ideas of order, of quiet, of sober well-established principles, of hoary usage and reverend custom. Every thing seems to be the growth of ages of regular and peaceful existence. The old church of remote architecture, with its low, massive portal; its Gothic tower; its windows rich with tracery and painted glass, in scrupulous preservation; its stately monuments of warriors and worthies of the olden time, ancestors of the present lords of the soil; its tombstones, recording successive generations of sturdy yeomanry, whose progeny still plough the same fields, and kneel at the same altar – the parsonage, a quaint irregular pile, partly antiquated, but repaired and altered in the tastes of various ages and occupants – the stile and foot-path leading from the churchyard, across pleasant fields, and along shady hedgerows, according to an immemorial right of way – the neighbouring village, with its venerable cottages, its public green sheltered by trees, under which the forefathers of the present race have sported – the antique family mansion, standing apart in some little rural domain, but looking down with a protecting air on the surrounding scene; all these common features of English landscape evince a calm and settled security, a hereditary transmission of homebred virtues and local attachments, that speak deeply and touchingly for the moral character of the nation.

WASHINGTON IRVING, *THE SKETCH-BOOK*
OF GEOFFREY CRAYON, GENT

Dear old Quarry Woods! with your narrow, climbing paths, and little winding glades, how scented to this hour you seem with memories of sunny summer days! How haunted are your shadowy vistas with the ghosts of laughing faces! how from your whispering leaves there softly fall the voices of long ago!

JEROME K. JEROME, *THREE MEN IN A BOAT*

The river – with the sunlight flashing from its dancing wavelets, gilding gold the grey-green beech-trunks, glinting through the dark, cool wood paths, chasing shadows o'er the shallows, flinging diamonds from the mill-wheels, throwing kisses to the lilies, wantoning with the weirs' white waters, silvering moss-grown walls and bridges, brightening every tiny townlet, making sweet each lane and meadow, lying tangled in the rushes, peeping, laughing, from each inlet, gleaming gay on many a far sail, making soft the air with glory – is a golden fairy stream.

JEROME K. JEROME, *THREE MEN IN A BOAT*

So Breaks The Sun

So breaks the sun earth's rugged chains,
Wherein rude winter bound her veins;
So grows both stream and source of price,
That lately fettered were with ice.
So naked trees get crispèd heads,
And coloured coats the roughest meads,
And all get vigour, youth, and spright,
That are but looked on by his light.

BEN JONSON

from Ode To Autumn

Season of mists and mellow fruitfulness,
Close bosom-friend of the maturing sun;
Conspiring with him how to load and bless
With fruit the vines that round the thatch-eaves run;
To bend with apples the mossed cottage-trees,
And fill all fruit with ripeness to the core;
To swell the gourd, and plump the hazel shells
With a sweet kernel; to set budding more,
And still more, later flowers for the bees,
Until they think warm days will never cease,
For Summer has o'er-brimmed their clammy cell.

JOHN KEATS

On the Grasshopper and the Cricket

The poetry of earth is never dead:
When all the birds are faint with the hot sun,
And hide in cooling trees, a voice will run
From hedge to hedge about the new-mown mead;
That is the Grasshopper's – he takes the lead
In summer luxury, – he has never done
With his delights; for when tired out with fun
He rests at ease beneath some pleasant weed.
The poetry of earth is ceasing never:
On a lone winter evening, when the frost
Has wrought a silence, from the stove there shrills
The Cricket's song, in warmth increasing ever,
And seems to one in drowsiness half lost,
The Grasshopper's among some grassy hills.

JOHN KEATS

84

from Araluen

River, myrtle rimmed, and set
Deep amongst unfooted dells –
Daughter of grey hills of wet,
Born by mossed and yellow wells;

Now that soft September lays
Tender hands on thee and thine,
Let me think of blue-eyed days,
Star-like flowers and leaves of shine!

Cities soil the life with rust;
Water banks are cool and sweet;
River, tired of noise and dust,
Here I come to rest my feet.

Now the month from shade to sun
Fleets and sings supremest songs,
Now the wilful wood-winds run
Through the tangled cedar throngs.

HENRY KENDALL

Trees

I think that I shall never see
A poem lovely as a tree.

A tree whose hungry mouth is prest
Against the sweet earth's flowing breast;

A tree that looks at God all day,
And lifts her leafy arms to pray;

A tree that may in summer wear
A nest of robins in her hair;

Upon whose bosom snow has lain;
Who intimately lives with rain.

Poems are made by fools like me,
But only God can make a tree.

JOYCE KILMER

To sit with a dog on a hillside on a glorious
afternoon is to be back in Eden, where doing
nothing was not boring – it was peace.

MILAN KUNDERA

It was beautiful spring weather… Each day the sun rose earlier and set later. It was dawn by three in the morning, and twilight lingered till nine at night. The whole long day was a blaze of sunshine. The ghostly winter silence had given way to the great spring murmur of awakening life. This murmur arose from all the land, fraught with the joy of living. It came from the things that lived and moved again, things which had been as dead and which had not moved during the long months of frost. The sap was rising in the pines. The willows and aspens were bursting out in young buds. Shrubs and vines were putting on fresh garbs of green. Crickets sang in the nights, and in the days all manner of creeping, crawling things rustled forth into the sun. Partridges and woodpeckers were booming and knocking in the forest. Squirrels were chattering, birds singing, and overhead honked the wild-fowl driving up from the south in cunning wedges that split the air.

From every hill slope came the trickle of running water, the music of unseen fountains. All things were thawing, bending, snapping.

JACK LONDON, *CALL OF THE WILD*

An April Day

When the warm sun, that brings
Seed-time and harvest, has returned again,
'T is sweet to visit the still wood, where springs
The first flower of the plain.

I love the season well,
When forest glades are teeming with bright forms,
Nor dark and many-folded clouds foretell
The coming-on of storms.

From the earth's loosened mould
The sapling draws its sustenance, and thrives;
Though stricken to the heart with winter's cold,
The drooping tree revives.

The softly-warbled song
Comes from the pleasant woods, and coloured wings
Glance quick in the bright sun, that moves along
The forest openings.

When the bright sunset fills
The silver woods with light, the green slope throws
Its shadows in the hollows of the hills,
And wide the upland glows.

And when the eve is born,
In the blue lake the sky, o'er-reaching far,
Is hollowed out and the moon dips her horn,
And twinkles many a star.

Inverted in the tide

Stand the grey rocks, and trembling shadows throw,

And the fair trees look over, side by side,

And see themselves below.

Sweet April! many a thought

Is wedded unto thee, as hearts are wed;

Nor shall they fail, till, to its autumn brought,

Life's golden fruit is shed.

HENRY WADSWORTH LONGFELLOW

Woods in Winter

When winter winds are piercing chill,
And through the hawthorn blows the gale,
With solemn feet I tread the hill,
That overbrows the lonely vale.

O'er the bare upland, and away
Through the long reach of desert woods,
The embracing sunbeams chastely play,
And gladden these deep solitudes.

Where, twisted round the barren oak,
The summer vine in beauty clung,
And summer winds the stillness broke,
The crystal icicle is hung.

Where, from their frozen urns, mute springs
Pour out the river's gradual tide,
Shrilly the skater's iron rings,
And voices fill the woodland side.

Alas! how changed from the fair scene,
When birds sang out their mellow lay,
And winds were soft, and woods were green,
And the song ceased not with the day!

But still wild music is abroad,
Pale, desert woods! within your crowd;
And gathering winds, in hoarse accord,
Amid the vocal reeds pipe loud.

Chill airs and wintry winds! my ear
Has grown familiar with your song;
I hear it in the opening year,
I listen, and it cheers me long.

HENRY WADSWORTH LONGFELLOW

Rest is not idleness, and to lie sometimes on the grass under trees on a summer's day, listening to the murmur of the water, or watching the clouds float across the sky, is by no means a waste of time.

JOHN LUBBOCK, *THE USE OF LIFE*

In February

Now in the dark of February rains,
Poor lovers of the sunshine, spring is born,
The earthy fields are full of hidden corn,
And March's violets bud along the lanes;

Therefore with joy believe in what remains.
And thou who dost not feel them, do not scorn
Our early songs for winter overworn,
And faith in God's handwriting on the plains.

'Hope' writes he, 'Love' in the first violet,
'Joy,' even from Heaven, in songs and winds and trees;
And having caught the happy words in these
While Nature labours with the letters yet,
Spring cannot cheat us, though her hopes be broken,
Nor leave us, for we know what God hath spoken.

GEORGE MACDONALD

As far as the eye can reach it extends, a heaving, swelling sea of green as regular and continuous as that produced by the heaths of Scotland. The sculpture of the landscape is as striking in its main lines as in its lavish richness of detail; a grand congregation of massive heights with the river shining between, each carved into smooth, graceful folds without leaving a single rocky angle exposed, as if the delicate fluting and ridging fashioned out of metamorphic slates had been carefully sandpapered. The whole landscape showed design, like man's noblest sculptures. How wonderful the power of its beauty! Gazing awe-stricken, I might have left everything for it. Glad, endless work would then be mine tracing the forces that have brought forth its features, its rocks and plants and animals and glorious weather. Beauty beyond thought everywhere, beneath, above, made and being made forever. I gazed and gazed and longed and admired until the dusty sheep and packs were far out of sight, made hurried notes and a sketch, though there was no need of either, for the colours and lines and expression of this divine landscape-countenance are so burned into mind and heart they surely can never grow dim.

JOHN MUIR, *MY FIRST SUMMER IN THE SIERRA*

Climb the mountains and get their good tidings. Nature's peace will flow into you as sunshine flows into trees. The winds will blow their own freshness into you, and the storms their energy, while cares will drop away from you like the leaves of Autumn.

JOHN MUIR, *OUR NATIONAL PARKS*

People from a planet without flowers
would think we must be mad with
joy... to have such things about us.

IRIS MURDOCH, *A FAIRLY HONOURABLE DEFEAT*

Who Has Seen the Wind?

Who has seen the wind?
Neither I nor you.
But when the leaves hang trembling,
The wind is passing through.

Who has seen the wind?
Neither you nor I.
But when the trees bow down their heads,
The wind is passing by.

CHRISTINA ROSSETTI

Sunshine is delicious, rain is refreshing, wind braces us up, snow is exhilarating; there is really no such thing as bad weather, only different kinds of good weather.

JOHN RUSKIN

To be interested in the changing
seasons is a happier state of mind than
to be hopelessly in love with spring.

George Santayana

… unfrequented woods,
I better brook than flourishing peopled towns,
Here can I sit alone, unseen of any,
And to the nightingale's complaining notes,
Tune my distresses, and record my woes.

WILLIAM SHAKESPEARE, *THE TWO GENTLEMEN OF
VERONA*

I spent the following day roaming through the valley…
The abrupt sides of vast mountains were before me;
the icy wall of the glacier overhung me; a few shattered
pines were scattered around; and the solemn silence of
this glorious presence-chamber of imperial nature was
broken only by the brawling waves or the fall of some
vast fragment, the thunder sound of the avalanche or
the cracking, reverberated along the mountains, of the
accumulated ice, which, through the silent working
of immutable laws, was ever and anon rent and torn,
as if it had been but a plaything in their hands. These
sublime and magnificent scenes afforded me the greatest
consolation that I was capable of receiving. They elevated
me from all littleness of feeling, and although they did

not remove my grief, they subdued and tranquillised it. In some degree, also, they diverted my mind from the thoughts over which it had brooded for the last month. I retired to rest at night; my slumbers, as it were, waited on and ministered to by the assemblance of grand shapes which I had contemplated during the day. They congregated round me; the unstained snowy mountain-top, the glittering pinnacle, the pine woods, and ragged bare ravine, the eagle, soaring amidst the clouds – they all gathered round me and bade me be at peace.

MARY SHELLEY, *FRANKENSTEIN*

from Summer And Winter

It was a bright and cheerful afternoon,
Towards the end of the sunny month of June,
When the north wind congregates in crowds
The floating mountains of the silver clouds
From the horizon – and the stainless sky
Opens beyond them like eternity.
All things rejoiced beneath the sun; the weeds,
The river, and the corn-fields, and the reeds;
The willow leaves that glanced in the light breeze,
And the firm foliage of the larger trees.

PERCY BYSSHE SHELLEY

Ode Written on the First of December

Tho' now no more the musing ear
Delights to listen to the breeze
That lingers o'er the green wood shade,
I love thee Winter! well.

Sweet are the harmonies of Spring,
Sweet is the Summer's evening gale,
Pleasant the Autumnal winds that shake
The many-colour'd grove.

And pleasant to the sober'd soul
The silence of the wintry scene,
When Nature shrouds herself, entranced
In deep tranquillity.

Not undelightful now to roam
The wild heath sparkling on the sight;
Not undelightful now to pace
The forest's ample rounds,

And see the spangled branches shine,
And mark the moss of many a hue
That varies the old tree's brown bark,
Or o'er the grey stone spreads.

The cluster'd berries bright
Amid the bright hollies gay green leaves;
The ivy round the leafless oak
Clasps its full foliage close.

So Virtue diffident of strength
Clings to Religion's firmer aid,
And by Religion's aid upheld
Endures calamity.

Nor void of beauties now the spring,
Whose waters hid from summer-sun
Have sooth'd the thirsty pilgrim's ear
With more than melody.

The green moss shines with icy glare,
The long grass bends its spear-like form;
And lovely is the silvery scene
When faint the sun-beams smile.

Reflection too may love the hour
When Nature, hid in Winter's grave,
No more expands the bursting bud
Or bids the flowret bloom,

For Nature soon in Spring's best charms
Shall rise reviv'd from Winter's grave.
Again expand the bursting bud,
And bid the flowret re-bloom.

ROBERT SOUTHEY

Over the Land is April

Over the land is April,
Over my heart a rose;
Over the high, brown mountain
The sound of singing goes.
Say, love, do you hear me,
Hear my sonnets ring?
Over the high, brown mountain,
Love, do you hear me sing?

By highway, love, and byway
The snows succeed the rose.
Over the high, brown mountain
The wind of winter blows.
Say, love, do you hear me,
Hear my sonnets ring?
Over the high, brown mountain
I sound the song of spring,
I throw the flowers of spring.
Do you hear the song of spring?
Hear you the songs of spring?

ROBERT LOUIS STEVENSON

It is not so much for its beauty that the forest
makes a claim upon men's hearts, as for
that subtle something, that quality of air, that
emanation from old trees, that so wonderfully
changes and renews a weary spirit.

Robert Louis Stevenson, 'Morality'

Trees are the earth's endless effort
to speak to the listening heaven.

RABINDRANATH TAGORE

Wild Asters

In the spring I asked the daisies
If his words were true,
And the clever, clear-eyed daisies
Always knew.

Now the fields are brown and barren,
Bitter autumn blows,
And of all the stupid asters
Not one knows.

SARA TEASDALE

from Early Spring

Once more the Heavenly Power
Makes all things new,
And domes the red-plowed hills
With loving blue;
The blackbirds have their wills,
The throstles too.

{...}

Past, Future glimpse and fade
Through some slight spell,
A gleam from yonder vale,
Some far blue fell;
And sympathies, how frail,
In sound and smell!

Till at thy chuckled note,
Thou twinkling bird,
The fairy fancies range,
And, lightly stirred,
Ring little bells of change
From word to word.

For now the Heavenly Power
Makes all things new,
And thaws the cold, and fills
The flower with dew;
The blackbirds have their wills,
The poets too.

ALFRED, LORD TENNYSON

from The Brook

I come from haunts of coot and hern,
I make a sudden sally
And sparkle out among the fern,
To bicker down a valley.

By thirty hills I hurry down,
Or slip between the ridges,
By twenty thorpes, a little town,
And half a hundred bridges.

Till last by Philip's farm I flow
To join the brimming river,
For men may come and men may go,
But I go on for ever.

I chatter over stony ways,

In little sharps and trebles,

I bubble into eddying bays,

I babble on the pebbles.

With many a curve my banks I fret

By many a field and fallow,

And many a fairy foreland set

With willow-weed and mallow.

I chatter, chatter, as I flow

To join the brimming river,

For men may come and men may go,

But I go on for ever.

ALFRED, LORD TENNYSON

from April

The sweetest thing, I thought

At one time, between earth and heaven

Was the first smile

When mist has been forgiven

And the sun has stolen out,

Peered, and resolved to shine at seven

On dabbled lengthening grasses,

Thick primroses and early leaves uneven,

When earth's breath, warm and

humid, far surpasses

The richest oven's, and loudly rings 'cuckoo'

And sharply the nightingale's

'tsoo, tsoo, tsoo, tsoo':

To say 'God bless it' was all that I could do.

EDWARD THOMAS

One such footpath I remember, that could be seen falling among woods and rising over hills, faint and winding, and disappearing at last, like a vision of the perfect quiet life. We started once along it, over one of the many fair little Oxford bridges, one that cleared the stream in three graceful leaps of arching stone. The hills were cloudy with woods in the heat. On either hand, at long distances apart, lay little grey houses under scalloped capes of thatch, and here and there white houses, like children of that sweet land – *albi circum ubera nati*. For the most part we saw only the great hawthorn hedge, which gave us the sense of a companion always abreast of us, yet always cool and fresh as if just setting out. It was cooler when a red-hot bicyclist passed by. A sombre river, noiselessly sauntering seaward, far away dropped with a murmur, among leaves, into a pool. That sound alone made tremble the glassy dome of silence that extended miles on miles. All things were lightly powdered with gold, by a lustre that seemed to have been sifted through gauze. The hazy sky, striving to be blue, was reflected as purple in the waters. There, too, sunken and motionless, lay amber willow leaves; some floated down. Between the sailing leaves, against the false sky, hung the willow shadows, shadows of willows overhead, with waving foliage, like the train of a bird of paradise. Everywhere the languid perfumes of corruption. Brown leaves laid their fingers on the cheek as they fell; and here and there the hoary reverse of a willow leaf gleamed in the crannied bases of the trees. A plough, planted in mid-field, was curved like the wings of a bird alighting.

EDWARD THOMAS, *OXFORD*

October

The green elm with the one great bough of gold
Lets leaves into the grass slip, one by one, –
The short hill grass, the mushrooms
small milk-white,
Harebell and scabious and tormentil,
That blackberry and gorse, in dew and sun,
Bow down to; and the wind travels too light
To shake the fallen birch leaves from the fern;
The gossamers wander at their own will.
At heavier steps than birds' the squirrels scold.
The rich scene has grown fresh again and new
As Spring and to the touch is not more cool
Than it is warm to the gaze; and now I might
As happy be as earth is beautiful,

Were I some other or with earth could turn
In alternation of violet and rose,
Harebell and snowdrop, at their season due,
And gorse that has no time not to be gay.
But if this be not happiness, – who knows?
Some day I shall think this a happy day,
And this mood by the name of melancholy
Shall no more blackened and obscured be.

EDWARD THOMAS

Now I yearn for one of those old, meandering, dry uninhabited roads, which lead away from towns, which lead us away from temptation… where you may forget in what country you are travelling; where no farmer can complain that you are treading down his grass… where travellers are not too often to be met; where my spirit is free; where the walls and fences are not cared for; where your head is more in heaven than your feet are on Earth; which have long reaches where you can see the approaching traveller half a mile off and be prepared for him… where you can walk and think with least obstruction, there being nothing to measure progress by… There I can walk, and recover the lost child that I am without any ringing of a bell.

HENRY DAVID THOREAU, *A WRITER'S JOURNAL*

Nature

O Nature! I do not aspire
To be the highest in thy choir, –
To be a meteor in thy sky,
Or comet that may range on high;
Only a zephyr that may blow
Among the reeds by the river low;
Give me thy most privy place
Where to run my airy race.

In some withdrawn, unpublic mead
Let me sigh upon a reed,
Or in the woods, with leafy din,
Whisper the still evening in:
Some still work give me to do, –
Only – be it near to you!

For I'd rather be thy child
And pupil, in the forest wild,
Than be the king of men elsewhere,
And most sovereign slave of care;
To have one moment of thy dawn,
Than share the city's year forlorn.

HENRY DAVID THOREAU

I felt my spirits rise when I had got off the road into the open fields, and the sky had a new appearance. I stepped along more buoyantly. There was a warm sunset over the wooded valleys, a yellowish tinge on the pines. Reddish dun-coloured clouds like dusky flames stood over it… Before I walked in the ruts of travel; now I adventured.

HENRY DAVID THOREAU, *A WRITER'S JOURNAL*

Walking

To walk abroad is, not with eyes,
But thoughts, the fields to see and prize;
Else may the silent feet,
Like logs of wood,
Move up and down, and see no good
Nor joy nor glory meet.

Ev'n carts and wheels their place do change,
But cannot see, though very strange
The glory that is by;
Dead puppets may
Move in the bright and glorious day,
Yet not behold the sky.

And are not men than they more blind,
Who having eyes yet never find
The bliss in which they move;
Like statues dead
They up and down are carried
Yet never see nor love.

To walk is by a thought to go;
To move in spirit to and fro;
To mind the good we see;
To taste the sweet;
Observing all the things we meet
How choice and rich they be.

To note the beauty of the day,
And golden fields of corn survey;
Admire each pretty flow'r
With its sweet smell;
To praise their Maker, and to tell
The marks of his great pow'r.

To fly abroad like active bees,
Among the hedges and the trees,
To cull the dew that lies
On ev'ry blade,
From ev'ry blossom; till we lade
Our minds, as they their thighs.

Observe those rich and glorious things,
The rivers, meadows, woods, and springs,
The fructifying sun;
To note from far
The rising of each twinkling star
For us his race to run.

A little child these well perceives,
Who, tumbling in green grass and leaves,
May rich as kings be thought,
But there's a sight
Which perfect manhood may delight,
To which we shall be brought.

While in those pleasant paths we talk,
'Tis that tow'rds which at last we walk;
For we may by degrees
Wisely proceed
Pleasures of love and praise to heed,
From viewing herbs and trees.

THOMAS TRAHERNE

It was a beautiful summer afternoon, at that delicious period of the year when summer has just burst forth from the growth of spring; when the summer is yet but three days old, and all the various shades of green which nature can put forth are still in their unsoiled purity of freshness. The apple blossoms were on the trees, and the hedges were sweet with May. The cuckoo at five o'clock was still sounding his soft summer call with unabated energy, and even the common grasses of the hedgerows were sweet with the fragrance of their new growth. The foliage of the oaks was complete, so that every bough and twig was clothed; but the leaves did not yet hang heavy in masses, and the bend of every bough and the tapering curve of every twig were visible through their light green covering. There is no time of the year equal in beauty to the first week in summer; and no colour which nature gives, not even the gorgeous hues of autumn, which can equal the verdure produced by the first warm suns of May.

ANTHONY TROLLOPE, *FRAMLEY PARSONAGE*

What is it that confers the noblest delight? What is that which swells a man's breast with pride above that which any other experience can bring to him? Discovery! To know that you are walking where none others have walked.

MARK TWAIN, *THE INNOCENTS ABROAD*

It was the cool grey dawn, and there was a delicious sense of repose and peace in the deep pervading calm and silence of the woods. Not a leaf stirred; not a sound obtruded upon great Nature's meditation. Beaded dewdrops stood upon the leaves and grasses...

Now, far away in the woods a bird called; another answered; presently the hammering of a woodpecker was heard. Gradually the cool dim grey of the morning whitened, and as gradually sounds multiplied and life manifested itself. The marvel of Nature shaking off sleep and going to work unfolded itself to the musing boy. A little green worm came crawling over a dewy leaf, lifting two-thirds of his body into the air from time to time and 'sniffing around', then proceeding again... Now a procession of ants appeared, from nowhere in particular, and went about their labours; one struggled manfully by with a dead spider five times as big as itself in its arms, and lugged it straight up a tree-trunk. A brown spotted lady-bug climbed the dizzy height of a grass blade, and Tom bent down close to it and said, 'Lady-bug, lady-bug, fly away home, your house is on fire, your children's alone,' and she took wing and went off to see about it – which did not surprise the boy, for he knew of old that this insect was credulous about conflagrations, and he had practised upon its simplicity more than once. A tumblebug came next, heaving sturdily at its ball, and Tom touched the creature, to see it shut its legs against its body and pretend to be dead. The birds were fairly rioting by this time… All Nature was wide awake and stirring, now; long lances of sunlight pierced down through the dense foliage far and near, and a few butterflies came fluttering upon the scene.

MARK TWAIN, *THE ADVENTURES OF TOM SAWYER*

I roamed the countryside
searching for answers to
things I did not understand.

Leonardo da Vinci

In nature, nothing is perfect and everything is perfect. Trees can be contorted, bent in weird ways, and they're still beautiful.

ALICE WALKER

After this whirlwind Mr Hoopdriver paid his reckoning and – being now a little rested about the muscles of the knees – resumed his saddle and rode on in the direction of Ripley, along an excellent but undulating road... And once he almost ran over something wonderful, a little, low, red beast with a yellowish tail, that went rushing across the road before him. It was the first weasel he had ever seen in his cockney life. There were miles of this, scores of miles of this before him, pinewood and oak forest, purple, heathery moorland and grassy down, lush meadows, where shining rivers wound their lazy way, villages with square-towered, flint churches, and rambling, cheap, and hearty inns, clean, white, country towns, long downhill stretches, where one might ride at one's ease (overlooking a jolt or so), and far away, at the end of it all, – the sea.

H. G. WELLS, *THE WHEELS OF CHANCE*

The early mist had vanished and the fields lay like a silver shield under the sun. It was one of the days when the glitter of winter shines through a pale haze of spring. Every yard of the road was alive with Mattie's presence, and there was hardly a branch against the sky or a tangle of brambles on the bank in which some bright shred of memory was not caught. Once, in the stillness, the call of a bird in a mountain ash was so like her laughter that his heart tightened and then grew large; and all these things made him see that something must be done at once.

EDITH WHARTON, *ETHAN FROME*

They drove slowly up the road between fields glistening under the pale sun, and then bent to the right down a lane edged with spruce and larch. Ahead of them, a long way off, a range of hills stained by mottlings of black forest flowed away in round white curves against the sky. The lane passed into a pine-wood with boles reddening in the afternoon sun and delicate blue shadows on the snow. As they entered it the breeze fell and a warm stillness seemed to drop from the branches with the dropping needles. Here the snow was so pure that the tiny tracks of wood-animals had left on it intricate lace-like patterns, and the bluish cones caught in its surface stood out like ornaments of bronze.

EDITH WHARTON, *ETHAN FROME*

from Give Me the Splendid, Silent Sun

Give me the splendid silent sun,
with all his beams full-dazzling;
Give me juicy autumnal fruit, ripe
and red from the orchard;
Give me a field where the
unmow'd grass grows;
Give me an arbor, give me the trellis'd grape;
Give me fresh corn and wheat – give me
serene-moving animals, teaching content.

WALT WHITMAN

from The Worship of Nature

The harp at Nature's advent strung
Has never ceased to play;
The song the stars of morning sung
Has never died away.

[...]

The green earth sends its incense up
From many a mountain shrine;
From folded leaf and dewy cup
She pours her sacred wine.

The mists above the morning rills
Rise white as wings of prayer;
The altar-curtains of the hills
Are sunset's purple air.

The winds with hymns of praise are loud,
Or low with sobs of pain, –
The thunder-organ of the cloud,
The dropping tears of rain.

With drooping head and branches crossed
The twilight forest grieves,
Or speaks with tongues of Pentecost
From all its sunlit leaves.

The blue sky is the temple's arch,
Its transept earth and air,
The music of its starry march
The chorus of a prayer.

So Nature keeps the reverent frame
With which her years began,
And all her signs and voices shame
The prayerless heart of man.

JOHN GREENLEAF WHITTIER

A March Snow

Let the old snow be covered with the new:
The trampled snow, so soiled, and stained, and sodden.
Let it be hidden wholly from our view
By pure white flakes, all trackless and untrodden.
When Winter dies, low at the sweet Spring's feet
Let him be mantled in a clean, white sheet.

Let the old life be covered by the new:
The old past life so full of sad mistakes,
Let it be wholly hidden from the view
By deeds as white and silent as snow-flakes.

Ere this earth life melts in the eternal Spring
Let the white mantle of repentance fling
Soft drapery about it, fold on fold,
Even as the new snow covers up the old.

ELLA WHEELER WILCOX

Bleak Weather

Dear Love, where the red lilies blossomed and grew
The white snows are falling;
And all through the woods where I wandered with you
The loud winds are calling;
And the robin that piped to us tune upon tune,
Neath the oak, you remember,
O'er hill-top and forest has followed the June
And left us December.
He has left like a friend who is true in the sun
And false in the shadows;
He has found new delights in the land where he's gone,
Greener woodlands and meadows.
Let him go! what care we? let the snow shroud the lea,
Let it drift on the heather;

We can sing through it all: I have you, you have me.
And we'll laugh at the weather.
The old year may die and a new year be born
That is bleaker and colder:
It cannot dismay us; we dare it, we scorn,
For our love makes us bolder.
Ah, Robin! sing loud on your far distant lea,
You friend in fair weather!
But here is a song sung that's fuller of glee,
By two warm hearts together.

ELLA WHEELER WILCOX

Magdalen Walks

The little white clouds are racing over the sky,
And the fields are strewn with the
gold of the flower of March,
The daffodil breaks under foot, and the tasselled larch
Sways and swings as the thrush goes hurrying by.

A delicate odour is borne on the
wings of the morning breeze,
The odour of deep wet grass, and of
brown new-furrowed earth,
The birds are singing for joy of the Spring's glad birth,
Hopping from branch to branch on the rocking trees.

And all the woods are alive with the
murmur and sound of Spring,
And the rose-bud breaks into pink on the climbing briar,
And the crocus-bed is a quivering moon of fire
Girdled round with the belt of an amethyst ring.

And the plane to the pine-tree is
whispering some tale of love
Till it rustles with laughter and
tosses its mantle of green,
And the gloom of the wych-elm's
hollow is lit with the iris sheen
Of the burnished rainbow throat and
the silver breast of a dove.

See! the lark starts up from his bed in the meadow there,
Breaking the gossamer threads and the nets of dew,
And flashing adown the river, a flame of blue!
The kingfisher flies like an arrow, and wounds the air.

OSCAR WILDE

from A Narrow Girdle of Rough Stones and Crags

A narrow girdle of rough stones and crags,
A rude and natural causeway, interposed
Between the water and a winding slope
Of copse and thicket, leaves the eastern shore
Of Grasmere safe in its own privacy:
And there myself and two beloved Friends,
One calm September morning, ere the mist
Had altogether yielded to the sun,
Sauntered on this retired and difficult way.
– Ill suits the road with one in haste; but we
Played with our time; and, as we strolled along,
It was our occupation to observe
Such objects as the waves had tossed ashore –
Feather, or leaf, or weed, or withered bough,
Each on the other heaped, along the line
Of the dry wreck. And, in our vacant mood,
Not seldom did we stop to watch some tuft
Of dandelion seed or thistle's beard,

That skimmed the surface of
the dead calm lake,
Suddenly halting now – a lifeless stand!
And starting off again with freak as sudden;
In all its sportive wanderings, all the while,
Making report of an invisible breeze
That was its wings, its chariot, and its horse,
Its playmate, rather say, its moving soul.
– And often, trifling with a privilege
Alike indulged to all, we paused, one now,
And now the other, to point out, perchance
To pluck, some flower or water-weed, too fair
Either to be divided from the place
On which it grew, or to be left alone
To its own beauty.

WILLIAM WORDSWORTH

151

I Wandered Lonely as a Cloud

I wandered lonely as a cloud
That floats on high o'er vales and hills,
When all at once I saw a crowd,
A host, of golden daffodils;
Beside the lake, beneath the trees,
Fluttering and dancing in the breeze.

Continuous as the stars that shine
And twinkle on the milky way,
They stretched in never-ending line
Along the margin of a bay:
Ten thousand saw I at a glance,
Tossing their heads in sprightly dance.

The waves beside them danced; but they

Out-did the sparkling waves in glee:

A poet could not but be gay,

In such a jocund company:

I gazed – and gazed – but little thought

What wealth the show to me had brought:

For oft, when on my couch I lie

In vacant or in pensive mood,

They flash upon that inward eye

Which is the bliss of solitude;

And then my heart with pleasure fills,

And dances with the daffodils.

WILLIAM WORDSWORTH

Written in March

While resting on the bridge at the foot of Brother's Water

The cock is crowing,
The stream is flowing,
The small birds twitter,
The lake doth glitter,
The green field sleeps in the sun;
The oldest and youngest
Are at work with the strongest;
The cattle are grazing,
Their heads never raising;
There are forty feeding like one!
Like an army defeated
The snow hath retreated,

And now doth fare ill
On the top of the bare hill;
The ploughboy is whooping – anon – anon:
There's joy in the mountains;
There's life in the fountains;
Small clouds are sailing,
Blue sky prevailing;
The rain is over and gone!

William Wordsworth

from The Eagle and the Mole

If you would keep your soul
From spotted sight or sound,
Live like the velvet mole:
Go burrow underground.

And there hold intercourse
With roots of trees and stones,
With rivers at their source,
And disembodied bones.

ELINOR WYLIE

The Wild Swans at Coole

The trees are in their autumn beauty,
The woodland paths are dry,
Under the October twilight the water
Mirrors a still sky;
Upon the brimming water among the stones
Are nine and fifty swans.

The nineteenth Autumn has come upon me
Since I first made my count;
I saw, before I had well finished,
All suddenly mount
And scatter wheeling in great broken rings
Upon their clamorous wings.

I have looked upon those brilliant creatures,
And now my heart is sore.
All's changed since I, hearing at twilight,
The first time on this shore,
The bell-beat of their wings above my head,
Trod with a lighter tread.

Unwearied still, lover by lover,
They paddle in the cold,
Companionable streams or climb the air;
Their hearts have not grown old;
Passion or conquest, wander where they will,
Attend upon them still.

But now they drift on the still water
Mysterious, beautiful;
Among what rushes will they build,
By what lake's edge or pool
Delight men's eyes, when I awake some day
To find they have flown away?

W. B. YEATS

I know the joy of fishes in the
river through my own joy, as I go
walking along the same river.

ZHUANGZI

If you're interested in finding out more about our books,
find us on Facebook at **Summersdale Publishers**
and follow us on Twitter at **@Summersdale**.

www.summersdale.com